Journey in Ryhme: Poems of Reflection

Reflective Poems, Volume 1

Dr Andrew C S Koh

Published by Dr Andrew C S Koh Publishing, 2024.

Copyright

Scan QR code to claim a free e-book

Dr Andrew C S Koh

Table of Contents

To my beloved wife, Wai Yin, whose love and unwavering support have been the foundation of everything I do.

To my sons, who have brought joy and purpose into my life.

To my daughters-in-law, who have enriched our family with their warmth and kindness.

To my grandsons and granddaughters, the light of my life, who remind me daily of the beauty and wonder of the world.

Above all, to the glory of God, whose grace has guided me through every step of my journey.

Finally, this book is for you.

from the back page

"In the rhythm of surrender and the rhyme of grace,

I find that even the longest journeys will

lead me home when God sets the pace."

Foreword

In a world brimming with noise and distraction, poetry emerges as a sanctuary, a haven where the soul can breathe, reflect, and discover meaning amidst the chaos. *Journey in Rhyme* invites readers on a deep journey through human experiences, capturing joy, sorrow, love, and reflection beautifully.

Throughout our journey in life, we experience a wide range of emotions, each one waiting to be expressed. The poems in this collection reflect the poet's personal experiences and reveal universal truths that connect us all. With striking imagery and sincere language, these verses resonate powerfully, encouraging us to pause and reflect on our own experiences.

This collection goes beyond just words; it powerfully shows how poetry connects us. Each poem offers valuable insights that promote reflection and relate to everyone. *Journey in Rhyme* beautifully encourages thought and emotion, allowing readers to find comfort in shared experiences.

Embarking on this poetic journey invites you to explore the profound depths of reflection and the transformative magic of language. Let the rhythm of each line carry you away, and may the poems echo within your soul long after you've closed the book.

Step into a realm brimming with introspection, emotion, and lyrical beauty.

David Lim Sui Ming

July 2025

Dr Andrew C S Koh

Preface

Journey in Rhyme is a labor of love, a collection of poems born from moments of inspiration, introspection, and life's myriad experiences. As a writer, I have often found solace in the written word, using poetry to navigate the complexities of emotion and the beauty of existence. This book encapsulates my journey, inviting readers to explore the landscapes of thought and feeling that define our shared humanity.

The poems within these pages are a tapestry woven from the threads of my life, each piece reflecting a unique facet of my experiences. They touch on themes of faith, life, love, nature, travel, Bible, and others. In writing these poems, I sought to capture fleeting moments, to freeze them in time, allowing readers to connect with their own reflections and emotions.

This collection is as much about my voice as it is about yours. Poetry, in its essence, is an invitation to share in a collective experience, to find familiarity in the unfamiliar, and to discover the profound in the everyday. I hope that through these poems, you find echoes of your own journey and a sense of companionship in the exploration of life's intricate tapestry.

As you read, I encourage you to pause and reflect, to let the words wash over you, and to embrace the emotions they evoke. Poetry has the power to illuminate the hidden corners of our hearts, offering comfort and understanding in moments of solitude.

Thank you for joining me on this journey of reflection. I hope these poems resonate, inspire, and encourage you to embrace the beauty of life's moments, both big and small.

With gratitude,

Dr Andrew C S Koh

July 2025

Dr Andrew C S Koh

Testimonials

I love poetry, and this book really brings poetry to life for me. It's inspirational. It reminds me of much of the music I get to sing. It's prayerful and thoughtful, using many of our common prayers and Bible stories. It makes me want to get back to writing poetry. These poems are beautiful in their simplicity, sincerity, and in pure prayerful love. Highly recommended. Jennifer Surdam.

This is a beautiful collection of poems that are about the Holy Land sites or a life in Christ. Inspirational. Rowan E Creech.

A selection of poems on various themes that tells its own story which gives thought to the reader. An enjoyable collection. Recommended, Sharmani Jeyaram.

This is a very interesting collection of poetry. I particularly enjoyed the poetic descriptions of places in Israel, especially the ones I have visited. Thoroughly enjoyable. Recommended, Linda Foster.

Dr Andrew C S Koh

Chapter 1
From Farm to Surgery

Life takes root in the farm,
Leaves that sprout in bright colors and vibrant hues,
Nature's balm is so soothing and calm,
A haven green beneath my feet.
As seasons change, so do trials,
From the embrace of earth to something slow,
The hands of a surgeon are so delicate and kind,
Now, tend to my body, mind, and soul.
Once I planted and watched the seeds grow,
Healing now comes in a new flow,
With steady hand, and careful grace,
They worked to fix the seeds in place.
Art and skill merged in the gardens and clinics,
God's hand is in the gardens and clinics,
The surgeon's light and the garden's peace,
Together, mend, and restore the broken piece.

Dr Andrew C S Koh

Chapter 2
Peace

Softly whispering peace,
A gentle calm in deepest sleep,
It calms down storms and stills the sea.
Grace is a gift of free will and serenity.
True happiness is not found in wealth and gains,
You are not marked by joy or pain,
The flame is always burning inside,
Even fame and strife cannot change the mind.
When shadows and worry grow,
The gentle sunrise begins to glow,
A silent strength, a quiet cheer,
Bring us together and bring us near.
This peace is my rest,
To bless my spirit and soul,
The sacred calm always bless,
And peace is all I do.

Dr Andrew C S Koh

Chapter 3
Two Photos on the Wall

Two photos are hung on the wall,
Captured moments, time's soft call,
One of old faces,
Of smiles frozen in time.
Another, more recent, but just as bright,
A younger face, untouched by years,
Two worlds collide in shared daylight,
Where memory whispers through silent tears.
One is wise and weathered by time,
Beneath distant skies where losses chime,
The other dreams with hope unseen,
Softly whispering what might have been,
Though the road is bold, the heart feels light,
The future glows with gentle light.
Two pictures framed in one true story,
A fragile path through grief and glory.
Each moment stitched with joy and pain,
Of hearts that find their way again.

Dr Andrew C S Koh

Chapter 4
Humility

Humility is a gentle grace,
Invisible, yet lights each place,
It doesn't boast or try to gain acclaim,
But softly glows, without a name.
It bends like grass beneath the breeze,
It strength is found in yielding ease,
No need for pride or grand display,
What truly grows won't fade away.
Serving hands and a softened heart,
It is the most pure, authentic part,
It bows the strong and lifts the meek,
A healer for the soul we seek.
Allow me to walk in humble grace,
Unseen content, day by day,
The quiet path is deep and true,
I walk in grace in all I do.

Dr Andrew C S Koh

Chapter 5
A Time for Everything

There is a time to laugh and a time for tears,
A joy that can chase away all fears,
There is a time to gather and a time to part,
But always keep joy within your heart.
There is a time for sowing and a moment for seed,
A time to let life's rivers lead,
There is a time to grow and a moment to rest.
A chance to reflect on what's truly best.
There is a time to speak and moments of peace,
When we are weak, it is a time for strength's release,
There is a time for war and a moment for peace,
When all our worries must finally cease.
Every season serves a purpose true,
Each moment weaves life's grander view,
Let's welcome each new dawn that sings,
For every season holds its wings.

Dr Andrew C S Koh

Chapter 6
This World is not our Home

The sky is grey, and the shadows wide deep,
Each day drifts by, a moment we must keep,
With weary hearts and souls that long for light,
We seek out peace to make the darkness bright.
This world is filled with trials, loss and tears,
When joy and sorrow mingle with our fears,
Yet, hope still shines through all the pain and strife,
And dreams still whisper promises of life.
Every mountain we climb is a test we face,
Every rhyme and rhythm, a fleeting trace
We journey on as time drifts by,
This path is made for you and I
Let us cherish the treasures that light our way,
Let laughter and love fill each day,
Though life holds trials as we roam,
We walk with hope as this world's not our home.

Dr Andrew C S Koh

Chapter 7
From Stethoscope to Wisdom

From the stethoscope to wisdom's way,
A healer's light, both night and day,
Hands once steady, sharp, and sure,
Now pause to wonder, to endure.
I felt life's beats beneath my hands,
Every story written, carefully planned,
In whispered rooms where hope appear,
I learned that love must cast out fear,
Not pride alone but grace I found.
In silent strength, where hearts resound,
Healing hands, a sacred art,
A lifelong calling from the heart.
A path ordained by God alone,
Marked by trials, tears, and love,
Through joy and pain, I've come to see,
That wisdom grows in humility.
The tools remain, the hours still call,
But purpose shifts within it all,
A new path forms, both kind and true,
As stethoscopes give way to view,
The deeper ways of healing grace,

Where wisdom takes the stethoscope's place.

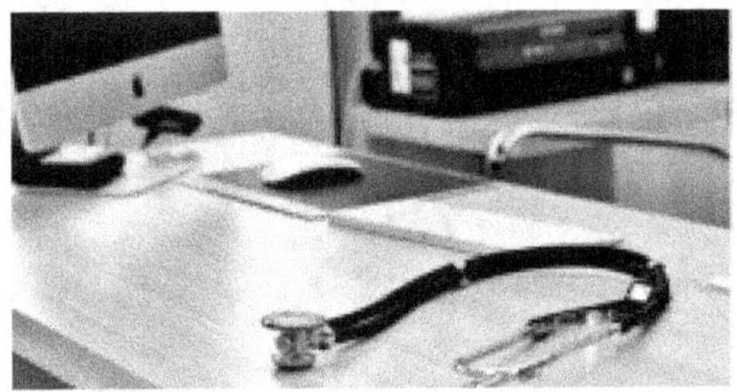

Dr Andrew C S Koh

Chapter 8
A Doctor's Calling

A strong call, a purpose bright and clear,
To heal, to hold, to draw lives near,
In rooms where pain and hope reside,
A doctor stands with skill and pride.
With listening ears and steady hand,
They help each soul to rise and stand,
Each breath, each beat, a sacred cue,
For every life brings something new.
Through sleepless nights and endless days,
They walk the long unwavering way,
Though trials, tests, and burdens weigh,
Their quiet strength won't drift away.
It's more than science, art, or skill,
It's heart and soul, a steadfast will,
A sacred call that won't grow dim,
To heal, to serve, to care, to give.

Dr Andrew C S Koh

Chapter 9
Knowledge

A spark ignites and the mind set free,
To chase the truth, to learn, to be,
A never-ending quest unfolds,
In silent halls with books and scrolls.
Not merely facts or wisdom's name,
But deeper truth, a wisdom's flame,
For every question plants a seed,
That blossoms into thought and deed.
It sharpens the sight and stirs the soul,
A light that makes the seeker whole,
A star that guides through darkest skies,
To hidden truths where wonder lies.
Knowledge, fierce, yet gently kind,
It shapes the heart and molds the mind,
Beyond mere thoughts or scholar's fame
It's in the heart; it lights the flame.

Dr Andrew C S Koh

Chapter 10
Reflections of a Doctor

I stood in the quiet halls with sterile lights,
before life and night,
With trembling fingers and steadfast resolve,
I learned how to heal, mend, and solve.
I watched hearts break and mend,
The stories of a thousand lives are woven to bear,
Every breath is a steady beat,
I walked the line where life and death meet.
The stethoscope, my faithful guide,
Beside his bed, I prayed and cried,
A heart laid bared, a soul in strain,
I offered hope through silent pain.
In the rush, the race, and the strife,
I discovered the pulse of my life,
Each soft smile and every tear,
I saw the reason why I am here.
My hands are still, the work now done,
The healing days have met their sun,
Yet, in the silence of the night,
I hear heartbeats flutter, soft, and light.
Although I've left the doctor's care,

Its presence lingers in the air,
Reflections deep, I carry on,
With heart and hope forever drawn.

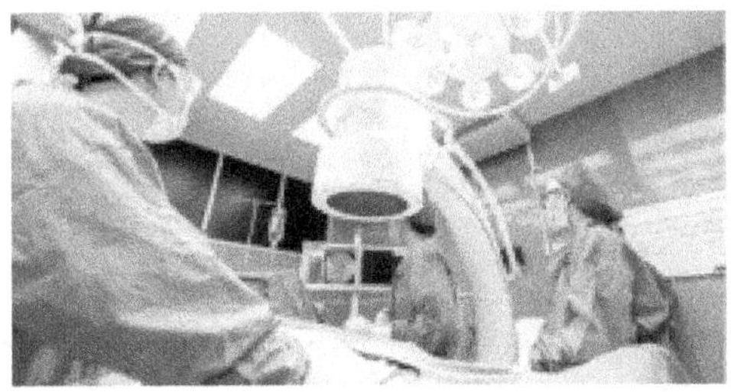

Dr Andrew C S Koh

Chapter 11
Tyranny of the Urgent

The clock ticks loud, a ruthless king,
Demanding tribute from everything.
Tasks stack high, they suffocate,
Each breath weighed down by heavy fate.
A voice insists, "Do it now!"
No room for rest, no time to bow.
But in the noise, I lose the best,
The sacred gift of peace and rest.
Urgency shouts, it steals my calm,
But what is gained if I lose my psalm?
I trade the still for rushing schemes,
And miss the quiet, holy dreams.
Duties drown the soul's soft cry,
The need to act comes flying by.
Yet like a cloud or shadow fast,
Such moments never seem to last.
But wisdom waits in silence deep,
In slower rhythms, hearts can keep.
I heard Him whisper through the storm:
"Be still, My child, let Me transform."
The world may clamor, loud with strife,
But peace is found in sacred life.

Urgent things may rule the day,
But Heaven's joy won't fade away.
In God's stillness, time expands,
No rushing clock, no harsh demands.
His strength is sure, unhurried, kind,
A deeper trust, a clearer mind.
So I will wait and not be swayed,
By fleeting hours or plans I made.
In silence, truth is gently stirred,
Life is built upon His Word.

Dr Andrew C S Koh

Chapter 12
Time

The river flows, both strong and true,
From morning's gold to evening's blue.
Moments slip like grains of sand,
Through eager hearts and open hands.
In youth, it runs both wild and wide,
A mystery none can quite confide.
But as it flows, it starts to slow,
And teaches more than we could know.
Time heals, it shapes, it gently bends,
A quiet guide, a faithful friend.
Our climb, our joy, each tear and trial,
All woven through each precious mile.
So hold each fleeting moment tight,
They pass like stars lost to the night.
For time once gone won't be replayed,
Its worth is found in how it's made.

Dr Andrew C S Koh

Chapter 13
Floating in the Dead Sea

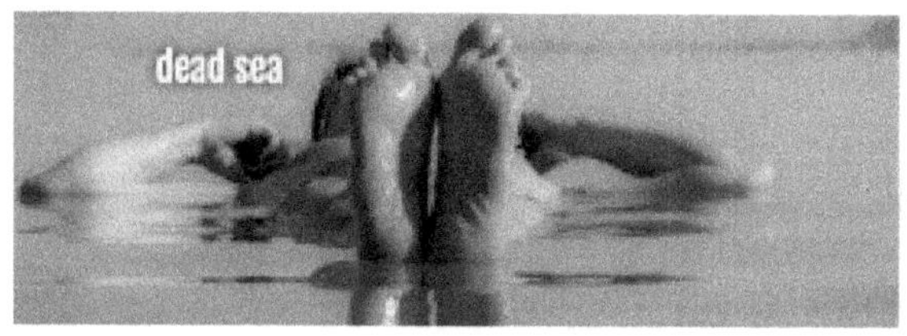

The Dead Sea rests in a gentle embrace,
Bathed in the golden sun's warm face.
Where sky and land in silence meet,
I float, weightless, in retreat.
On this ancient, timeless bed,
Cradled in stillness, softly led.
Like a leaf upon the sea,
I drift, unanchored, calm and free.
In salty depths, the shadows lift,
As moments pass in gentle drift.
Suspended 'tween the earth and sky,
I float in dreams that never die.
No effort here, no need to strive,
No rushing pulse, yet fully alive.
Peace surrounds on every side,
The noisy world now pushed aside.
Replaced by calm, a tranquil breath,
A soothing hush, a sacred depth.
In waters dense and still, I find
A quiet healing for the mind.
While floating close to eternity,

The sea becomes a mirror to me.
Horizons blur with every sway,
And time itself just melts away.
In this hush of quiet grace,
The Dead Sea is a sacred place.
A timeless space without a name,
Yet everything feels just the same.
Here, where life seems gently paused,
A silent song without a cause.
Floating in the Dead Sea's hold,
Is where I rest, where I unfold.

Dr Andrew C S Koh

Chapter 14
Covid 19

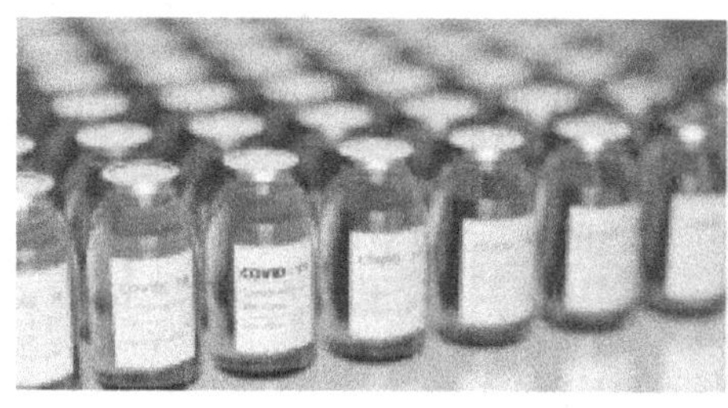

The land was swept by a silent wave,
A force unseen, yet deeply grave.
The streets grew still, the doors all closed,
A world on pause, not self-imposed.
The day wore masks and kept its space,
With longing etched on every face.
Though hearts grew tired, homes became light,
A refuge born from silent fight.
Doctors, nurses on the line,
Stood tall with courage, strong, divine.
With unseen scars and steadfast grace,
They shone like stars in darkest place.
For every loss, a price was paid,
Where grief and strength together stayed.
Communities, once torn, grew tight,
Fear gave way to hope and light.
We're healing now, though slow the pace,
Each step a sign of love's embrace.
A chapter closed, but truths remain,
That out of sorrow rises gain.

Each breath we take, a gift so dear,
A sign that love still draws us near.
The world renewed, its heart above,
Restored through grace, rebuilt by love.

Dr Andrew C S Koh

Chapter 15
Locked Down

The world withdrew in silent gloom,
Locked behind each shuttered room.
Once-crowded streets lay still and bare,
A hush replaced the city's flare.
Routines reset in muted grey,
As time stretched long from day to day.
Bound by rules we couldn't bend,
We found new truths we didn't intend.
Children's laughter, a fading sound,
As echoes of the past surround.
Normal scenes we held so tight
Now drift like dreams into the night.
Yet in the quiet, something grew,
A gentler way, a clearer view.
We reached through screens, wrote words with care,
Connection formed through silent prayer.
The seeds of grace, though buried deep,
Stirred in the still, began to creep.
With books and candles softly lit,
We found the peace where we once split.
Locked down, yet drawn to something higher,

Hearts warmed by an unseen fire.
And when the doors swing open wide,
A kinder world may rise with pride.

If you like what you are reading, consider leaving a review. Even a short review will be most appreciated. Scan the QR code to download a review copy.

Dr Andrew C S Koh

Chapter 16
The Joy of Writing

A blank page waits, so still, so pure,
A canvas vast, yet edges sure.
The heart takes flight with pen in hand,
To shape a world, to make it stand.
The wildest thoughts now dance with glee,
The truth unfolds and calls to me.
With every word, a spark takes flight,
And whispers bloom into shining light.
Each line becomes a path I tread,
A journey where the soul is led.
Through realms of thought I roam alone,
Yet joy and wonder gently grown.
In rhyme and verse, I find my place,
Beyond the world's relentless pace.
For here, where dreams and stories blend,
Even paper becomes a friend.
The secret joy of writing flows,
In every line, the spirit grows.
Exploring truth, both bold and bright,
Word after word, I walk in light.

Dr Andrew C S Koh

Chapter 17
Splendor of Angkor Wat

In the first light of dawn, a temple stands,
Crafted by ancient and devoted hands,
The towers of Angkor are serene and grand,
A breathtaking creation sculpted from hallowed sand.
Stone whispers stories of days gone by,
Concerning kings, gods and celestial bodies under the sky,
Exquisite carvings made with a master's care.
Tales that are profound, timeless, and rare.
Lotus blooms on waters clear,
The reflection of beauty calm and near,
The sun rays reflected on sandstone walls,
Halls adorned with a regal aura and shadowed calls.
Steps worn by many feet,
Resonate in rhythms sweet,
The mystery lingers in the vastness and deep,
In the sanctuaries where the spirits sleep.

Reflections

Dr Andrew C S Koh

Chapter 18
Splendid Taj Mahal

Bathed in lunar light, it gleams serene,
A masterpiece of marble in a silvery sheen.
The Taj Mahal, a vision of love so bright,
A monument crafted from passion's height.
By the tranquil banks of Yamuna's shore,
Its secrets flow like currents for evermore,
A timeless promise etched in the king's own tone,
For a bond that even death could not disown.
Spires reaching high and arches wide,
Echo the sorrows a soul can confide,
Delicate petals and jewels inlayed,
In stone's embrace, they serenely bide.
Sunrise bathes it with warm and gold,
A tale where dreams and hearts behold,
Yet in its silence lies a sigh,
As hearts entwine, their whispers fly.
Symbol of love, timeless grace,
A haven for the soul's embrace.
In every heartbeat, a story stays,
A reflection of timeless grace.

Dr Andrew C S Koh

Chapter 19
Timeless Forbidden City

Where emperors reigned and secrets lie,
Where history whispers and legends sigh.
A realm adorned with royal grace,
Shielded from the world's embrace.
Majestic dragons soar and glide,
Cloaked in darkness, watchful they bide.
In gilded chambers and emerald-lit rooms,
Whispers dance through shadowed gloom.
Expanses grand, where silence sings,
Echoes woven through time's delicate seams.
A kingdom's heartbeat in every stone,
Bound by fate, yet free to roam.
Time weaves its tale, yet walls remain,
A fortress blessed by dawn and rain,
Across the ages, tales unfold,
Of valor, glory, dreams, and gold.
The Forbidden City stands majestic and grand,
A marvel of history, a masterpiece spanned,
Through whispered tales and ancient lore,
A sanctuary lost in memories' shore.

Dr Andrew C S Koh

Chapter 20
Iconic Sistene Chapel

Adorned with whispers and diving grace,
Sistine Chapel, where heaven and artistry embrace.
A canvas extends gracefully from wall to dome,
In the realm of dreams, their spirits roam.
Michelangelo's brush soared to life,
Transforming stone into divine light.
Inspiration's flame, a gift refined,
In brilliant hues, delicate and bright.
Angels whisper and cherubs sing,
In sunlit chambers, their echoes ring.
Every brush a devotion, every hue bold,
A saga of spirit and colors unfold.
From Adam's touch to God's warm embrace,
A testament to divine grace,
A whispered prayer, a promise deep,
Where hearts ignite and dreams leap.
The Sistine Chapel, masterpiece of divine art,
A canvas where heaven and earth impart.
In each moment, eternity,
A captivating insight of God's own majesty.

Dr Andrew C S Koh

Chapter 21

Mischievous Tom Sawyer

Where the gentle waters flow and the willow leans,
Tom Sawyer dreams beneath the sunlit beams,
Barefoot dreamer with a twinkle bright,
On sun-kissed days and golden light.
A jaunty straw hat tilted, a playful grin,
Ready to create, he sparks joy within,
Fences painted with vibrant care,
Whispers of hope spun in the air.
Where echoes dance, beneath the beams,
As whispers linger, lost dreams gleam,
An unyielding companion to Huck, a rascal true,
Through tangled paths and daring escapades they flew.
The enchanting allure of a treasure on a haunted night,
With a heart ignited by unrestrained delight,
A soul unleashed, vibrant, untamed, alive,
In every scheme and dream revived.
The adventures of a young dreamer, a timeless tale,
Where dreams take flight and wonders never fail,
With hearts unbound by daring joys,
Innocent laughter, life's joyful boy.

Dr Andrew C S Koh

Chapter 22
Magical Disneyland

With magic that dances in every arc,
Awaits at Disneyland, where dreams embark,
A realm spun from fairy tales,
As joy resounds and wishes set sail.
Castles gleam in hues of light,
Their silhouettes dance in gentle twilight,
Laughter dances through every street,
In rhythms both bright and fleet.
Adventures beckon and dreams soar,
Each land is a tale waiting to unfold,
In the dance of dreams and laughter's song,
We uncover the world where hearts are strong.
Festive lights and dazzling fireworks' blaze,
Spark a wonder in every heart's embrace,
With every fleeting grin, a wish takes flight,
In visions that swirl with the stars' gentle light.
Disneyland, an enchanting land,
Where dreams come alive and smiles expand,
A realm where wonder knows no end,
And magic fills the air again.

Dr Andrew C S Koh

Chapter 23
Monet Museum

Where lilies dance on water's gleam,
Monet Museum, where art and nature's harmony beam,
A blossom's grace, a stream's soft glow,
Whispers gentle like the winds that blow.
Brushstrokes dance in light's embrace,
Colors whisper solace's trace,
Capturing moments in time and space,
Here, the colors sing, a vivid display,
Telling stories of beauty in a magical way.
In the twilight's embrace, the willow's sway,
As hues converge in a vibrant display,
In whispers soft where shadows belong,
The rhythm of dusk in a tender throng.
Every canvas pulsates, vibrant, deep, and profound,
Where colors twirl in dreams unbound,
In Monet's canvas, reflections gleam,
As light dances on the water's seam.
The Monet Museum, calm and still,
A sanctuary where dreams and colors spill,
Through shimmering lakes and vibrant skies,

A beauty perceived through compassionate eyes.

Dr Andrew C S Koh

Chapter 24
Picasso Museum

Amidst the echoes of vibrant forms and lines,
The essence of Picasso's creativity shines,
A realm reimagined by imagination bold,
Where dreams collide and tales unfold.
Visages contorted, shapes redefined,
Every canvas reflects a tumultuous mind,
From shadows that linger deep despair,
To brilliant sparks that twirl in air.
The brush strokes dance with passion's fire,
In each creation, a new desire,
Abstract visions and disconnected sights,
A cosmos of kaleidoscopic lights.
Sculptures emerge from earth and stone,
In every shape, a story shone,
An artist's heart, untamed and free,
Echoes of visions in a vibrant plea.
Picasso Museum, a destination vast,
Where imagination and color freely contrast.
In every shadow, life's spark was found,

A tribute to dreams unbound.

Dr Andrew C S Koh

Chapter 25
Van Gogh Museum

In the heart of Amsterdam, where colors bloom,
Van Gogh Museum, a haven of masterpieces to consume,
A sanctuary where imagination ignites,
Where artistry dances and passion takes flight.
Colors twirl in a vibrant sky,
In starry nights, as galaxies dance high.
Meadows of gold and sunflowers bright,
Each brushstroke sings of pure delight.
A restless heart with visions clear,
Transformed into memories we revere,
From vibrant strokes of passion's ease to cypress trees,
A soul entwined in twilight's tease.
Each shade reveals a tale untold,
Of laughter and loss in hues so bold,
In whispered echoes of the night and shadows cast,
A heartbeat through time to last.
The Van Gogh Museum, a destination deep,
Where dreams unfold and stories creep,
With each brushstroke, emotions embrace,

A canvas of souls, a legendary grace.

Dr Andrew C S Koh

Chapter 26
Enigmatic Mona Lisa

In the Louvre Museum, she silently waits,
A mystical gaze that enchants and creates,
The enigmatic masterpiece, with a smile so sly,
Conceals whispers hidden in every sigh.
Her gaze, luminous as stars, pierce the night,
A secret whispered through the quiet twilight,
With gentle strokes, a masterpiece unfurls,
A celestial grace that enchants the swirl.
Michelangelo's mastery of form and bright,
Her mystique weaves a captivating light,
Her essence sings of timeless art,
In her tranquil gaze, the moment last.
Enthralled, they gather a sea of awe,
Captivated by her grace, her quiet flaw,
With each glaze, a story we find,
Unveiling feelings, where dreams intertwine.
Mona Lisa, a timeless treasure revered,
A creation adored, both sought and revered,
In her silent allure, we come to see,
The whispers of art, a captivating mystery.

Dr Andrew C S Koh

Chapter 27
The Joy of Reading

In the hidden corners where stories swell,
The magic of stories begins to dwell,
Whispers of dreams with a gentle sigh,
Guiding souls to realms on high.
Pages flutter, dreams unfurled,
Endless journeys to be twirled,
From whispered lore to visions bright,
In every tale, a fire ignites.
Characters spring forth from the lines and lores,
Their hopes and visions, eternally soar,
With every turn of the page, new wonders unfold,
In realms of dreams, our spirits glow.
A crackling fire and a steaming cup,
In pages turned, we rise and sup,
Caught in the magic of words that chime,
Time suspends, in rhythms divine.
The joy of reading, a timeless grace,
A canvas of wonder, a soothing space,
A symphony of voices, emotions rare,
A tapestry of dreams woven with care.

Dr Andrew C S Koh

Chapter 29
Pandemic

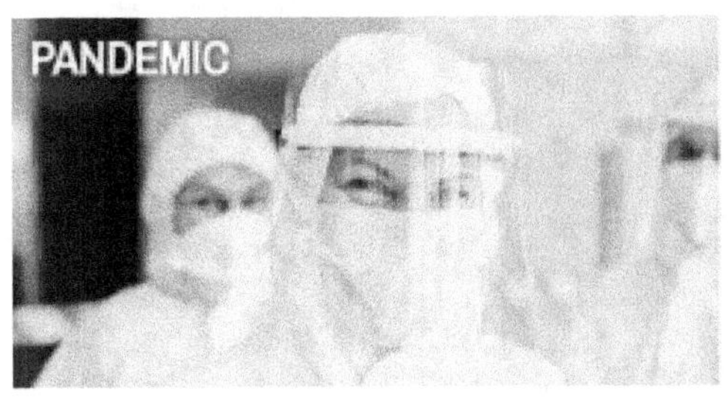

As silence wrapped us, a world in pause,
A quiet moment, a chance to pause,
In stillness shared, our spirits weep,
In solitude's embrace, our love grew deep.
A faint cough echoed distantly, a soft and muffled sound.
In fear we discovered the strength to stand our ground,
Masks hid the smiles we once wore,
Though distant, our hearts still reach for more.
Through expansive windows, the world outside,
Silent echoes in the streets where life once thrived,
And in stillness, our dreams ignite,
In hearts entwined, our spirits took flight.
Whispers of love and light that bridged,
The spaces that joined, our souls enriched,
In every moment, we found our place,
The dreams we wove, the gentle grace.
As we emerge from the shadows cast,
With wisdom gained, we stand steadfast.
With each setback, our strength bestows,
In the face of chaos, our courage flows.

Dr Andrew C S Koh

Chapter 30
Discovery

In solitude's embrace, when silence reigns,
A flame awakens, shattering the chains,
The joy of unearthing, horizons unknown,
Each step reveals where the wild winds have blown.
A sense of wonder beckons, drawing us near,
To explore the unknown we often fear,
With fearless hearts and spirits unconfined,
We uncover the mysteries that knowledge may find.
From far-off coastlines to the heavens above,
In nature's embrace, we learn to love,
In art's bright glow and time's vast stage,
We reveal timeless wisdom that transcends age.
Every step is a journey, and every question holds the key,
Opening the doors to what we can be,
In the embrace of curiosity, our spirits soar,
In the pursuit of wisdom, we discover much more.
Moments of clarity, a timeless refrain,
In whispers of life, in love's embrace,
While wandering through this magnificent place,
We savor the memories of every challenge we face.

Dr Andrew C S Koh

One Last Thing

Thank you once again for taking the time to explore my book. I genuinely hope it proved to be a rewarding experience for you. Your support means everything to me, and I am truly grateful to each reader who joins me on this journey. Together, we can cultivate a vibrant community of readers and writers united by our love for storytelling.

Each review contributes to a vibrant dialogue that enriches our literary experience. I look forward to hearing your thoughts and insights as we continue to explore the depths of creativity together. Your feedback is invaluable, and it inspires me to keep pushing the boundaries of my writing. Let's keep the conversation going and delve deeper into the stories that connect us all.

If you like what you are reading, consider leaving a review. Even a short review will be most appreciated. Scan the QR code to download a review copy.

Dr Andrew C S Koh

Dr Andrew C S Koh

If you like what you are reading, consider leaving a review. Even a short review will be most appreciated. Scan the QR code to download a review copy.

Dr Andrew C S Koh

Don't miss out!

Visit the website below and you can sign up to receive emails whenever Dr Andrew C S Koh publishes a new book. There's no charge and no obligation.

https://books2read.com/r/B-A-FMXV-VPDEF

Did you love *Journey in Ryhme: Poems of Reflection*? Then you should read *Whispers of Grace*[1] by Dr Andrew C S Koh!

[2]

Quiet moments. Honest prayers. Gentle truths. Let your heart be still and let grace speak.

In a world filled with noise, ***Whispers of Grace*** offers a calming voice of hope, healing, and reflection. This beautifully crafted collection of Christian and inspirational poetry invites you into a sacred space where faith is deepened and peace is renewed.

Whether you're navigating a season of struggle or simply seeking to draw closer to God, these poems will speak to the soul, gently reminding you of His constant presence and unchanging love. **Inside this uplifting collection, you'll find:**

---

1. https://books2read.com/u/bxXMjP

2. https://books2read.com/u/bxXMjP

Poems rooted in scripture and spiritual truthEncouragement for those facing trials or transitionsReflections on grace, forgiveness, and God's quiet strengthA comforting companion for prayer, journaling, or devotional time

Perfect for:

Devotional reading or quiet time

Gifts for loved ones needing encouragement

Those who enjoy faith-based poetry and reflection

Readers who crave peace, purpose, and God's presence

Let these verses wrap around your spirit like a gentle whisper from heaven.In every line, may you find light for your path and rest for your soul.

Read more at https://www.drandrewcskoh.com.

Also by Dr Andrew C S Koh

Bible Study
From Creation to Covenant
From Deceiver to Destiny: Jacob's Story
From Slavery to Freedom
From Man to Mission
From Slave to Brother
From Symbols to Salvation
From Legalism to Liberty
From Tribulation to Triumph

Daily Devotion
Manna of Life: Daily Devotion

Daily Devotions
Bread of Life Daily Devotions
Words of Eternal Life
Bread From Heaven: Daily Devotions
Light of the World Daily Devotions
Light of the World Daily Devotions
The Way, the Truth, and the Life

Rooted: A Daily Devotion to Deepen your Faith

Fiction
The Hourglass Paradox

Genesis
Understanding Genesis 1-11: From Adam to Abraham
Faith Journey of Abraham: Genesis 12-25
Life Story of Jacob: Genesis 26-36
The Story of Joseph: Genesis 37-50
From Pit to Palace

Gospels and Act
The Gospel According to Matthew
Daily Devotion Gospel of Mark
The Gospel According to Luke
Daily Devotion Gospel of John
Acts: Volume 1 and 2, From Jerusalem to Rome
From Galilee to Golgotha

Non Pauline and General Epistles
Hebrews: the Just Shall Live by Faith
1 John, 2 John, 3 John & Jude: a Verse by Verse Bible Study
General Epistles: 1 Peter, 2 Peter, James

Pauline Epistles
Romans: The Just Shall Live by Faith
1 Corinthians
2 Corinthians
1 Thessalonians, 2 Thessalonians, Philemon
Pastoral Epistles: 1 Timothy, 2 Timothy, Titus
Galatians: Justified by Faith in Jesus Christ
Philemon: Charge to the Master's Account

Prison Epistles
The Prison Epistles
Philippians: Rejoice Always in the Lord
Colossians: He is the Image of the Invisible God
Ephesians: Every Spiritual Blessings

Reflective Poems
Journey in Ryhme: Poems of Reflection
Whispers of Grace

Standalone
Apocalypse: Understanding the Book of Revelation
Expository Preaching
Memoirs of a Doctor
Moses: Let My People Go
Living Word Living Savior
From Stethoscope to Wisdom

Walking in His Footsteps: A Pilgrim's Journey
Mapping the Heart
The Forgotten Melody
Footprints in Time
From Love to Light
Time Traveller's Return
The hourglass Paradox

Watch for more at https://www.drandrewcskoh.com.

About the Author

Dr Andrew C S Koh a retired cardiologist, Bible teacher, and author of 50 titles. With a passion for making Scripture come alive, he blends theological insight with practical life application to help readers grow in faith and understanding. His writing reflects a deep commitment to God's Word, forged through decades of medical service, spiritual study, and personal devotion. Dr. Koh's works have encouraged believers around the world to walk closer with Christ and live out their calling with purpose and conviction.

Koh's unique perspective blends his extensive knowledge of the medical field with his deep theological insights. He studied theology at Laidlaw College in Auckland, New Zealand. He now calls Malaysia home, where he lives with his family. He made history in 2021 by setting a record in the Malaysia Book of Records for publishing the most books in a single year.

Whether he's teaching the Bible, creating digital content, or sharing his thoughts through various media, Dr. Koh's mission is clear: to make the Word of God accessible and relevant to everyday life. His works aim to inspire believers to grow deeper in their faith, live with purpose, and embrace the transformative power of God's love.

Link tree:

https://linktr.ee/andrewcskoh

https://books.drandrewcskoh.com/link-tree

free ebook:

https://storyoriginapp.com/giveaways/b295be58-7736-11ec-ac4b-e34d930c508e

Read more at https://www.drandrewcskoh.com.

About the Publisher

At *Dr. Andrew C. S. Koh Publishing*, we are dedicated to publishing Christ-centered, Scripture-based resources that edify the church, equip believers, and spread the gospel. Our aim is to glorify God by helping readers grow in biblical knowledge, spiritual maturity, and faithful living.

Rooted in Scripture and committed to the Great Commission, we exist to proclaim the timeless truths of God's Word through books, Bible studies, and resources for spiritual growth.

Whether you're a seeker, student, or seasoned believer, our mission is to help you deepen your faith and walk in the light of Christ.

Read more at https://www.drandrewcskoh.com.